pudgie parade

SHOPPING LIST

Yarn (Medium Weight) 4

- ☐ Black - 50 yards (45.5 meters)
- ☐ Red - 24 yards (22 meters)
- ☐ White - small amount

Crochet Hooks

- ☐ Size G (4 mm)
  or size needed for gauge

Additional Supplies

- ☐ Polyester fiberfill
- ☐ Yarn needle

STITCH GUIDE

SINGLE CROCHET 2 TOGETHER
(abbreviated sc2tog)
Pull up a loop in each of next 2 sts, YO and draw through all 3 loops on hook **(counts as one sc)** ***(Fig. A)***.

Fig. A

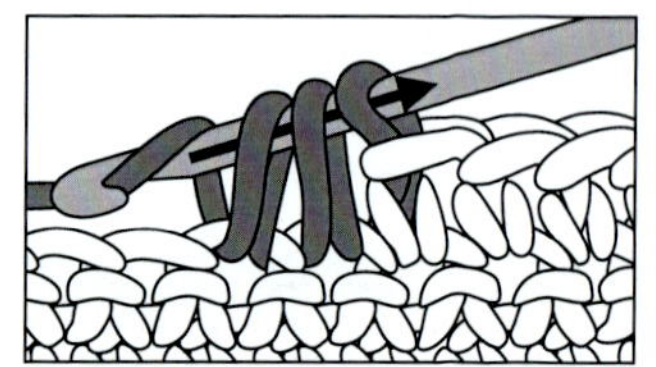

GAUGE INFORMATION

8 sc and 8 rows = 2" (5 cm)
Gauge Swatch: 2" (5 cm) square
Ch 9.
Row 1: Sc in second ch from hook and in each ch across: 8 sc.
Rows 2-8: Ch 1, turn; sc in each sc across.
Finish off.
Save time, check your gauge.

HEAD & BODY

Rnd 1 (Right side)**:** With Black, make an adjustable ring, work 6 sc in ring ***(Figs. 3a-d, pages 40 & 41)***; do **not** join, place marker to indicate the beginning of the round ***(Fig. 1, page 40)***.

Note: Loop a short piece of yarn around any stitch to mark Rnd 1 as **right** side.

Rnd 2: 2 Sc in each sc around: 12 sc.

Ladybug

EASY

Finished Length: Approx. 3½" (9 cm)

Rnd 3: (2 Sc in next sc, sc in next sc) around: 18 sc.

Rnds 4 and 5: Sc in each sc around; at end of Rnd 5, slip st in next sc.

Rnd 6: Sc in Back Loop Only of same st as slip st and each sc around ***(Fig. 6, page 42)***; do **not** join, place marker to indicate the beginning of the round.

Rnd 7: Working in both loops, (sc in next sc, 2 sc in next sc) around: 27 sc.

Rnd 8: Sc in each sc around.

Rnd 9: (Sc in next 8 sc, 2 sc in next sc) 3 times: 30 sc.

Rnd 10: (2 Sc in next sc, sc in next 4 sc) around: 36 sc.

Rnds 11 and 12: Sc in each sc around.

Rnd 13: (Sc2tog, sc in next 4 sc) around: 30 sc.

Rnd 14: Sc in each sc around.

Rnd 15: (Sc2tog, sc in next 4 sc) around: 25 sc.

Rnd 16: Sc in next 2 sc, sc2tog, (sc in next 3 sc, sc2tog) 4 times, sc in next sc: 20 sc.

Rnd 17: (Sc in next 2 sc, sc2tog) around: 15 sc.

Rnd 18: Sc in next 2 sc, sc2tog, (sc in next 3 sc, sc2tog) twice, sc in next sc: 12 sc.

Stuff piece with polyester fiberfill, shaping it like an egg.

Rnd 19: Sc2tog around; slip st in next sc, finish off leaving an 8" (20.5 cm) length for sewing: 6 sts.

Thread yarn needle with end and weave yarn through Front Loop Only of remaining sc to close ***(Fig. 6, page 42)***; secure end.

WINGS

First Wing

Row 1: With **right** side facing, having first round toward you and working in free loops of Rnd 5 ***(Fig. 5a, page 41)***, join Red with sc in first st ***(Fig. 2, page 40)***; sc in same st (sc in next st, 2 sc in next st) twice; leave remaining free loops unworked: 8 sc.

Row 2: Ch 1, turn; sc in each sc across.

Row 3: Ch 1, turn; sc in first 4 sc, 2 sc in next sc, sc in last 3 sc: 9 sc.

Row 4: Ch 1, turn; sc in each sc across.

Row 5: Ch 1, turn; sc in first 2 sc, 2 sc in next sc, sc in next 3 sc, 2 sc in next sc, sc in last 2 sc: 11 sc.

Row 6: Ch 1, turn; sc in first 3 sc, (2 sc in next sc, sc in next 3 sc) twice: 13 sc.

Rows 7 and 8: Ch 1, turn; sc in each sc across.

Row 9: Ch 1, turn; sc in first 9 sc, sc2tog, sc in last 2 sc: 12 sc.

Row 10: Ch 1, turn; sc in first 5 sc, sc2tog, sc in last 5 sc: 11 sc.

Row 11: Ch 1, turn; sc in first 3 sc, sc2tog, sc in next sc, sc2tog, sc in last 3 sc: 9 sc.

Row 12: Ch 1, turn; sc in first 2 sc, sc2tog, sc in next sc, sc2tog, sc in last 2 sc: 7 sc.

Row 13: Ch 1, turn; sc in first 3 sc, sc2tog, sc in last 2 sc: 6 sc.

Row 14: Ch 1, turn; sc in first 2 sc, sc2tog, sc in last 2 sc: 5 sc.

Row 15: Turn; skip first sc, sc2tog, sc in last 2 sc: 3 sc.

Row 16: Turn; skip first sc, sc2tog; finish off: one sc.

Second Wing

Row 1: With **right** side facing, having first round toward you and working in free loops of Rnd 5, join Red with sc in next unworked st from First Wing; sc in same st, (sc in next st, 2 sc in next st) twice; leave remaining free loops unworked: 8 sc.

Row 2: Ch 1, turn; sc in each sc across.

Row 3: Ch 1, turn; sc in first 3 sc, 2 sc in next sc, sc in last 4 sc: 9 sc.

Row 4: Ch 1, turn; sc in each sc across.

Row 5: Ch 1, turn; sc in first 2 sc, 2 sc in next sc, sc in next 3 sc, 2 sc in next sc, sc in last 2 sc: 11 sc.

Row 6: Ch 1, turn; sc in first 3 sc, (2 sc in next sc, sc in next 3 sc) twice: 13 sc.

Rows 7 and 8: Ch 1, turn; sc in each sc across.

Row 9: Ch 1, turn; sc in first 2 sc, sc2tog, sc in last 9 sc: 12 sc.

Row 10: Ch 1, turn; sc in first 5 sc, sc2tog, sc in last 5 sc: 11 sc.

Row 11: Ch 1, turn; sc in first 3 sc, sc2tog, sc in next sc, sc2tog, sc in last 3 sc: 9 sc.

Row 12: Ch 1, turn; sc in first 2 sc, sc2tog, sc in next sc, sc2tog, sc in last 2 sc: 7 sc.

Row 13: Ch 1, turn; sc in first 2 sc, sc2tog, sc in last 3 sc: 6 sc.

Row 14: Ch 1, turn; sc in first 2 sc, sc2tog, sc in last 2 sc: 5 sc.

Row 15: Turn; skip first sc, sc2tog, sc in last 2 sc: 3 sc.

Row 16: Turn; skip first sc, sc2tog; finish off: one sc.

SPOT (Make 10)

Rnd 1 (Right side)**:** With Black, make an adjustable ring, work 6 sc in ring; join with slip st to first sc, finish off leaving an 6" (15 cm) length for sewing.

Note: Mark Rnd 1 as **right** side.

LEG (Make 6)

With Black, ch 8; working in back ridges of ch *(**Fig. 4, page 41**)*, slip st in second ch from hook and in next 2 chs, (slip st, ch 1, slip st) in next ch (knee), slip st in last 3 chs; finish off leaving a 6" (15 cm) length for sewing.

ANTENNA (Make 2)

With Black, ch 5; working in back ridges of ch, pull up a loop in first ch (2 loops on hook), pull up a loop in second ch **and** draw through both loops on hook, slip st in next 3 chs; finish off leaving a 6" (15 cm) length for sewing.

FINISHING

Using Photo as a guide for placement and using long ends:

- Sew 5 Spots to each Wing.
- Sew Antennae to Head.
- With White and using French knots *(**Fig. 10, page 43**)*, add eyes.
- With White and using fly stitch *(**Fig. 11, page 44**)*, add mouth.

Designed by Linda A. Daley.

SHOPPING LIST

Yarn (Medium Weight) MEDIUM 4

- ☐ Yellow - 40 yards (36.5 meters)
- ☐ Black - 16 yards (14.5 meters)
- ☐ White - 10 yards (9 meters)

Crochet Hooks

- ☐ Size G (4 mm) **or** size needed for gauge

Additional Supplies

- ☐ Polyester fiberfill
- ☐ Yarn needle

STITCH GUIDE

SINGLE CROCHET 2 TOGETHER
(abbreviated sc2tog)

Pull up a loop in each of next 2 sts, YO and draw through all 3 loops on hook **(counts as one sc)** ***(Fig. A)***.

Fig. A

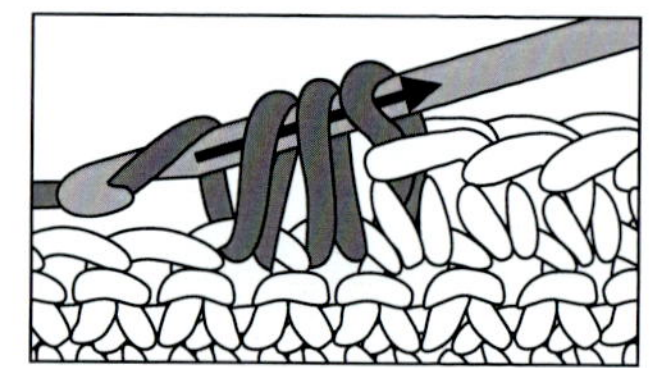

GAUGE INFORMATION

8 sc and 8 rows/rnds = 2" (5 cm)
Gauge Swatch: 2" (5 cm) square
Ch 9.
Row 1: Sc in second ch from hook and in each ch across: 8 sc.
Rows 2-8: Ch 1, turn; sc in each sc across.
Finish off.
Save time, check your gauge.

HEAD & BODY

Rnd 1 (Right side)**:** With Yellow, make an adjustable ring, work 6 sc in ring ***(Figs. 3a-d, pages 40 & 41)***; do **not** join, place marker to indicate the beginning of the round ***(Fig. 1, page 40)***.

Note: Loop a short piece of yarn around any stitch to mark Rnd 1 as **right** side.

Bee

EASY

Finished Length: Approx. 4" (10 cm)

Rnd 2: 2 Sc in each sc around: 12 sc.

Rnd 3: (Sc in next sc, 2 sc in next sc) around: 18 sc.

Rnd 4: (2 Sc in next sc, sc in next 2 sc) around: 24 sc.

Rnd 5: Sc in each sc around.

Rnd 6: (Sc in next 5 sc, 2 sc in next sc) around: 28 sc.

Rnds 7 and 8: Sc in each sc around.

Rnd 9: (Sc in next 6 sc, 2 sc in next sc) around changing to Black in last sc ***(Fig. 7a, page 42)***, drop Yellow to **wrong** side of work: 32 sc.

Rnd 10: Sc in each sc around changing to Yellow in last sc, drop Black to **wrong** side of work.

Rnd 11: Sc in each sc around changing to Black in last sc, drop Yellow to **wrong** side of work.

Rnd 12: Sc in each sc around changing to Yellow in last sc, drop Black to **wrong** side of work.

Rnd 13: (2 Sc in next sc, sc in next 7 sc) around changing to Black in last sc, drop Yellow to **wrong** side of work: 36 sc.

Rnds 14-16: Repeat Rnds 10-12.

Rnd 17: (Sc2tog, sc in next 7 sc) around changing to Black in last sc, cut Yellow: 32 sc.

Rnd 18: Sc in each sc around.

Rnd 19: (Sc in next 2 sc, sc2tog) around: 24 sc.

Rnd 20: Sc in each sc around.

Rnd 21: (Sc in next sc, sc2tog) around: 16 sc.

Rnd 22: Sc in each sc around.

Stuff piece with polyester fiberfill, shaping piece like an egg.

Rnd 23: Sc2tog around; slip st in next sc, finish off leaving an 8" (20.5 cm) length for sewing: 8 sts.

Thread yarn needle with end and weave yarn through Front Loops Only of remaining sc to close ***(Fig. 6, page 42)***; secure end.

WING (Make 2)

Rnd 1 (Right side)**:** With White, make an adjustable ring, work 5 sc in ring; do **not** join, place marker to indicate the beginning of the round.

Note: Mark Rnd 1 as **right** side.

Rnd 2: 2 Sc in each sc around: 10 sc.

Rnd 3: (Sc in next sc, 2 sc in next sc) around: 15 sc.

Rnd 4: Sc in next sc, (2 sc in next sc, sc in next sc) around: 22 sc.

Rnd 5: (Ch 1, slip st in next sc) 20 times; finish off leaving an 8" (20.5 cm) length for sewing.

FINISHING

Using Photo as a guide for placement and using long ends:

- Sew Wings across Rnds 9-11 on each side of Body.
- Using satin stitch ***(Fig. 8, page 43)***, add Black eyes.

Designed by Linda A. Daley.

SHOPPING LIST

Yarn (Medium Weight) 

- ☐ Brown - 50 yards (45.5 meters)
- ☐ Red - 10 yards (9 meters)
- ☐ Yellow - 3 yards (2.7 meters)
- ☐ Black - small amount

Crochet Hooks

- ☐ Size G (4 mm) **or** size needed for gauge

Additional Supplies

- ☐ Polyester fiberfill
- ☐ Yarn needle

STITCH GUIDE

SINGLE CROCHET 2 TOGETHER ***(abbreviated sc2tog)***

Pull up a loop in each of next 2 sts, YO and draw through all 3 loops on hook **(counts as one sc)** ***(Fig. A)***.

Fig. A

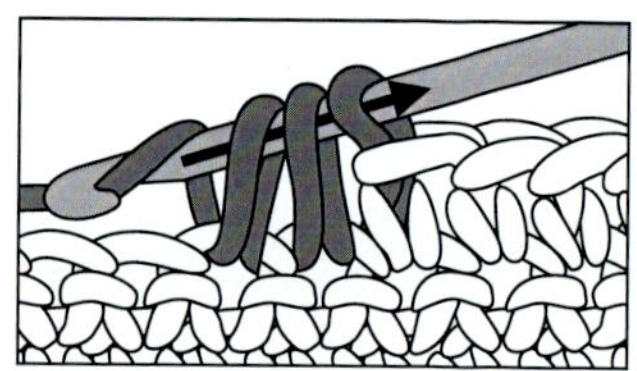

GAUGE INFORMATION

8 sc and 8 rows = 2" (5 cm)

Gauge Swatch: 2" (5 cm) square

Ch 9.

Row 1: Sc in second ch from hook and in each ch across: 8 sc.

Rows 2-8: Ch 1, turn; sc in each sc across.

Finish off.

Save time, check your gauge.

HEAD & BODY

Rnd 1 (Right side)**:** With Brown, make an adjustable ring, work 6 sc in ring ***(Figs. 3a-d, pages 40 & 41)***; do **not** join, place marker to indicate the beginning of the round ***(Fig. 1, page 40)***.

Note: Loop a short piece of yarn around any stitch to mark Rnd 1 as **right** side.

Rnd 2: 2 Sc in each sc around: 12 sc.

Birdy
EASY
Finished Height: Approx. 4" (10 cm)

Rnd 3: (Sc in next sc, 2 sc in next sc) around: 18 sc.

Rnd 4: (2 Sc in next sc, sc in next 2 sc) around: 24 sc.

Rnd 5: (Sc in next 5 sc, 2 sc in next sc) around: 28 sc.

Rnds 6-8: Sc in each sc around.

Rnd 9: (Sc in next 6 sc, 2 sc in next sc) around: 32 sc.

Rnds 10-12: Sc in each sc around.

Rnd 13: (2 Sc in next sc, sc in next 7 sc) around: 36 sc.

Rnds 14-16: Sc in each sc around.

Rnd 17: (Sc2tog, sc in next 7 sc) around: 32 sc.

Rnd 18: Sc in each sc around.

Rnd 19: (Sc in next 2 sc, sc2tog) around: 24 sc.

Rnd 20: Sc in each sc around.

Rnd 21: (Sc in next sc, sc2tog) around: 16 sc.

Rnd 22: Sc in each sc around.

Stuff piece with polyester fiberfill, shaping piece like an egg.

Rnd 23: Sc2tog around; slip st in next sc, finish off leaving an 8" (20.5 cm) length for sewing: 8 sts.

Thread yarn needle with end and weave yarn through Front Loops Only of remaining sc to close ***(Fig. 6, page 42)***; secure end.

BELLY

Rnd 1 (Right side)**:** With Red, make an adjustable ring, work 6 sc in ring; do **not** join, place marker to indicate the beginning of the round.

Note: Mark Rnd 1 as **right** side.

Rnd 2: 2 Sc in each sc around: 12 sc.

Rnd 3: (Sc in next sc, 2 sc in next sc) around: 18 sc.

Rnd 4: (2 Sc in next sc, sc in next 2 sc) around: 24 sc.

Rnd 5: (Sc in next 3 sc, 2 sc in next sc) around; slip st in next sc, finish off leaving a 12" (30.5 cm) length for sewing: 30 sts.

WING (Make 2)

Rnd 1 (Right side)**:** With Brown, make an adjustable ring, work 4 sc in ring; do **not** join, place marker to indicate the beginning of the round.

Note: Mark Rnd 1 as **right** side.

Rnd 2: 2 Sc in each sc around: 8 sc.

Rnd 3: Sc in each sc around.

Rnd 4: (Sc in next sc, 2 sc in next sc) around: 12 sc.

Rnd 5: Sc in each sc around.

Joining Row: Ch 1; flatten the Wing with the loop on hook at the fold and sts matching. Working through **both** loops of **both** sts, sc2tog, sc in next 2 sc, sc2tog; finish off leaving an 8" (20.5 cm) length for sewing.

BEAK

Rnd 1 (Right side)**:** With Yellow, make an adjustable ring, work 4 sc in ring; do **not** join, place marker to indicate the beginning of the round.

Note: Mark Rnd 1 as **right** side.

Rnd 2: (Sc in next sc, 2 sc in next sc) twice: 6 sc.

Rnd 3: (Sc in next sc, 2 sc in next sc) around; slip st in next sc, finish off leaving an 8" (20.5 cm) length for sewing: 9 sts.

FINISHING

Using photo as a guide for placement and using long ends:

- Sew Belly to Body, across Rnds 12-21.
- Sew Wings on each side of Body, angled across Rnds 10 and 11.
- Stuffing piece lightly with polyester fiberfill, sew Beak above the Belly across Rnds 8-11.
- Using satin stitch ***(Fig. 8, page 43)***, add Black eyes across Rnds 8 and 9, having 4 sts between eyes.

Designed by Linda A. Daley.

SHOPPING LIST

Yarn (Medium Weight) MEDIUM 4

- ☐ Brown - 35 yards (32 meters)
- ☐ White - 25 yards (23 meters)
- ☐ Yellow - 3 yards (2.7 meters)
- ☐ Black - small amount

Crochet Hooks

- ☐ Size G (4 mm)
  or size needed for gauge

Additional Supplies

- ☐ Polyester fiberfill
- ☐ Yarn needle

STITCH GUIDE

SINGLE CROCHET 2 TOGETHER
(abbreviated sc2tog)
Pull up a loop in each of next 2 sts, YO and draw through all 3 loops on hook **(counts as one sc)** ***(Fig. A)***.

Fig. A

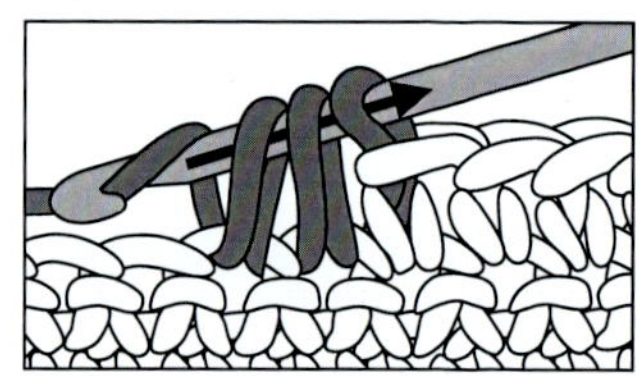

GAUGE INFORMATION

8 sc and 8 rows/rnds = 2" (5 cm)
Gauge Swatch: 2" (5 cm) square
Ch 9.
Row 1: Sc in second ch from hook and in each ch across: 8 sc.
Rows 2-8: Ch 1, turn; sc in each sc across.
Finish off.
Save time, check your gauge.

HEAD & BODY

Rnd 1 (Right side)**:** With White, make an adjustable ring, work 6 sc in ring ***(Figs. 3a-d, pages 40 & 41)***; do **not** join, place marker to indicate the beginning of the round ***(Fig. 1, page 40)***.

Note: Loop a short piece of yarn around any stitch to mark Rnd 1 as **right** side.

Rnd 2: 2 Sc in each sc around: 12 sc.

Eagle

EASY

Finished Height: Approx. 4 1/4" (10.75 cm)

Rnd 3: (Sc in next sc, 2 sc in next sc) around: 18 sc.

Rnd 4: (2 Sc in next sc, sc in next 2 sc) around: 24 sc.

Rnd 5: (Sc in next 5 sc, 2 sc in next sc) around: 28 sc.

Rnds 6-8: Sc in each sc around.

Rnd 9: (Sc in next 6 sc, 2 sc in next sc) around: 32 sc.

Rnd 10: (2 Sc in next sc, sc in next 7 sc) around: 36 sc.

Rnd 11: Sc in each sc around.

Rnd 12 (feathers)**:** Working in Front Loops Only *(Fig. 6, page 42)*, ★ sc in next sc, (hdc, dc, hdc) in next sc; repeat from ★ around changing to Brown in last hdc *(Fig. 7b, page 42)*, cut White: 18 feathers.

Rnd 13: With Brown and working **behind** the feathers and in free loops on Rnd 11 *(Fig. 5a, page 41)*, sc in each sc around: 36 sc.

Rnds 14-17: Sc in both loops of each sc around.

Rnd 18: (Sc2tog, sc in next 7 sc) around: 32 sc.

Rnd 19: Sc in each sc around.

Rnd 20: (Sc in next 2 sc, sc2tog) around: 24 sc.

Rnd 21: Sc in each sc around.

Rnd 22: (Sc in next sc, sc2tog) around: 16 sc.

Rnd 23: Sc in each sc around.

Stuff piece with polyester fiberfill, shaping piece like an egg.

Rnd 24: Sc2tog around; slip st in next sc, finish off leaving an 8" (20.5 cm) length for sewing: 8 sts.

Thread yarn needle with end and weave yarn through Front Loop Only of remaining sc to close *(Fig. 6, page 42)*; secure end.

BEAK

Rnd 1 (Right side)**:** With Yellow, make an adjustable ring, work 4 sc in ring; do **not** join, place marker to indicate the beginning of the round.

Note: Mark Rnd 1 as **right** side.

Rnd 2: (Sc in next sc, 2 sc in next sc) twice: 6 sc.

Rnd 3: (Sc in next sc, 2 sc in next sc) 3 times: 9 sc.

Rnd 4: Sc in each sc around; slip st in next sc, finish off leaving an 8" (20.5 cm) length for sewing.

Stuff Beak lightly with polyester fiberfill.

WING (Make 2)

Rnd 1 (Right side)**:** With Brown, make an adjustable ring, work 4 sc in ring; do **not** join, place marker to indicate the beginning of the round.

Note: Mark Rnd 1 as **right** side.

Rnd 2: 2 Sc in each sc around: 8 sc.

Rnd 3: Sc in each sc around.

Rnd 4: (Sc in next sc, 2 sc in next sc) around: 12 sc.

Rnds 5 and 6: Sc in each sc around.

Joining Row: Ch 1; flatten the Wing with the loop on hook at the fold and sts matching. Working through **both** loops of **both** sts, sc2tog, sc in next 2 sc, sc2tog; finish off leaving an 8" (20.5 cm) end for sewing: 4 sc.

FINISHING

Using Photo as a guide for placement and using long ends:

- Sew Wings on each side of Body (below feathers), between Rnds 13 and 14.
- Sew Beak to Body above the feathers.
- Using satin stitch ***(Fig. 8, page 43)***, add Black eyes across Rnds 5 and 6, leaving 3 sts between eyes.

SHOPPING LIST

Yarn (Medium Weight) 

- ☐ Black - 50 yards (45.5 meters)
- ☐ White - 10 yards (9 meters)
- ☐ Gold - 10 yards (9 meters)

Crochet Hooks

- ☐ Size G (4 mm)
  or size needed for gauge

Additional Supplies

- ☐ Polyester fiberfill
- ☐ Yarn needle

STITCH GUIDE

SINGLE CROCHET 2 TOGETHER
(abbreviated sc2tog)
Pull up a loop in each of next 2 sts, YO and draw through all 3 loops on hook **(counts as one sc)** ***(Fig. A)***.

Fig. A

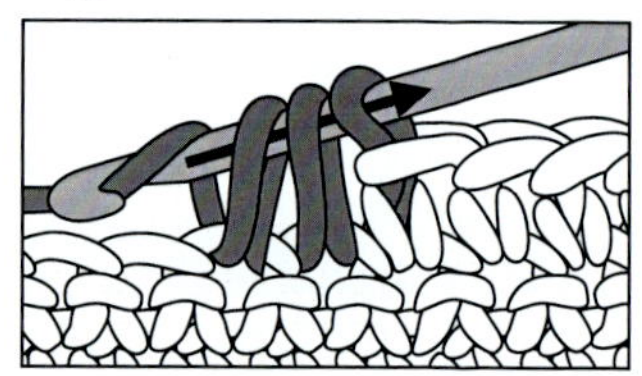

GAUGE INFORMATION

8 sc and 8 rows/rnds = 2" (5 cm)
Gauge Swatch: 2" (5 cm) square
Ch 9.
Row 1: Sc in second ch from hook and in each ch across: 8 sc.
Rows 2-8: Ch 1, turn; sc in each sc across.
Finish off.
Save time, check your gauge.

HEAD & BODY

Rnd 1 (Right side)**:** With Black, make an adjustable ring, work 6 sc in ring ***(Figs. 3a-d, pages 40 & 41)***; do **not** join, place marker to indicate the beginning of the round ***(Fig. 1, page 40)***.

Note: Loop a short piece of yarn around any stitch to mark Rnd 1 as **right** side.

Penguin

EASY

Finished Height: Approx. 4" (10 cm)

Rnd 2: 2 Sc in each sc around: 12 sc.

Rnd 3: (Sc in next sc, 2 sc in next sc) around: 18 sc.

Rnd 4: (2 Sc in next sc, sc in next 2 sc) around: 24 sc.

Rnd 5: (Sc in next 5 sc, 2 sc in next sc) around: 28 sc.

Rnds 6-8: Sc in each sc around.

Rnd 9: (Sc in next 6 sc, 2 sc in next sc) around: 32 sc.

Rnds 10-12: Sc in each sc around.

Rnd 13: (2 Sc in next sc, sc in next 7 sc) around: 36 sc.

Rnds 14-16: Sc in each sc around.

Rnd 17: (Sc2tog, sc in next 7 sc) around: 32 sc.

Rnd 18: Sc in each sc around.

Rnd 19: (Sc in next 2 sc, sc2tog) around: 24 sc.

Rnd 20: Sc in each sc around.

Rnd 21: (Sc in next sc, sc2tog) around: 16 sc.

Rnd 22: Sc in each sc around.

Stuff piece with polyester fiberfill, shaping piece like an egg.

Rnd 23: Sc2tog around; slip st in next sc, finish off leaving an 8" (20.5 cm) length for sewing: 8 sts.

Thread yarn needle with end and weave yarn through Front Loop Only of remaining sts to close ***(Fig. 6, page 42)***; secure end.

BELLY

Rnd 1 (Right side)**:** With White, ch 5; 2 sc in second ch from hook, hdc in next ch, 2 dc in next ch, 5 dc in last ch; working in free loops of beginning ch ***(Fig. 5b, page 42)***, 2 dc in next ch, hdc in next ch, 2 sc in next ch; do **not** join, place marker to indicate the beginning of the round: 15 sts.

Note: Mark Rnd 1 as **right** side.

Rnd 2: 2 Sc in next st, hdc in next 2 sts, 2 hdc in next st, 2 dc in each of next 7 sts, 2 hdc in next st, hdc in next 2 sts, slip st in next st; do **not** finish off: 25 sts.

EYE PATCH

Foundation Row: Sc in next sc, 2 sc in next sc, sc in next hdc, slip st in next hdc; do **not** finish off: 5 sts.

First Side

Row 1 (Wrong side)**:** Turn; skip first slip st, (hdc, dc) in next sc, (dc, hdc) in next sc, slip st in next sc, leave last sc unworked.

Row 2: Ch 1, turn; skip first slip st, sc in next hdc, 2 sc in next dc, sc in next dc, slip st in next hdc, ch 1, slip st in same hdc on Body as last slip st of Foundation Row; finish off.

Second Side

Row 1: With **wrong** side facing, join White with slip st in first unworked st after First Side; (hdc, dc) in next st, (dc, hdc) in next st, slip st in next hdc.

Row 2: Ch 1, turn; skip first slip st, sc in next hdc, 2 sc in next dc, sc in next dc, slip st in next hdc, ch 1, slip st in same st on Body as joining slip st; finish off.

BEAK

Rnd 1 (Right side)**:** With Gold, make an adjustable ring, work 3 sc in ring; do **not** join, place marker to indicate the beginning of the round.

Note: Mark Rnd 1 as **right** side.

Rnd 2: Sc in next sc, 2 sc in next sc, sc in next sc: 4 sc.

Rnd 3: 2 Sc in next sc, sc in next 3 sc: 5 sc.

Rnd 4: Sc in each sc around.

Rnd 5: Sc in next sc, (2 sc in next sc, sc in next sc) twice: 7 sc.

Rnd 6: Sc in each sc around; slip st in next sc, finish off leaving an 8" (20.5 cm) length for sewing.

WING (Make 2)

Rnd 1 (Right side)**:** With Black, make an adjustable ring, work 4 sc in ring; do **not** join, place marker to indicate the beginning of the round.

Note: Mark Rnd 1 as **right** side.

Rnd 2: (2 Sc in next sc, sc in next sc) twice: 6 sc.

Rnd 3: Sc in each sc around.

Rnd 4: (2 Sc in next sc, sc in next sc) 3 times: 9 sc.

Rnd 5: Sc in next 4 sc, 2 sc in next sc, sc in next 4 sc: 10 sc.

Rnds 6-8: Sc in each sc around.

Joining Row: Ch 1; flatten Wing with the ch at the fold and sts matching. Working through **both** loops of **both** sides, sc2tog twice, sc in last sc; finish off leaving an 8" (20.5 cm) length for sewing.

FEET

Row 1 (Right side)**:** With Gold, ch 5; sc in second ch from hook and in each ch across: 4 sc.

Note: Mark Row 1 as **right** side.

Row 2: Ch 1, turn; 2 sc in first sc, sc in next 2 sc, 2 sc in last sc: 6 sc.

Row 3: Ch 1, turn; 2 sc in first sc, sc in next sc, 2 sc in each of next 2 sc, sc in next sc, 2 sc in last sc; do **not** finish off: 10 sc.

First Foot

Row 1 (Wrong side)**:** Ch 1, turn; skip first sc, hdc in next 4 sc, leave remaining 5 sc unworked: 4 hdc.

Row 2: Ch 2, turn; (dc, ch 2, slip st) in first hdc, (slip st, ch 2, dc, ch 2, slip st) in each of next 2 hdc, slip st in last hdc; finish off.

Second Foot

Row 1: With **wrong** side facing, join Gold with slip st in first unworked sc after First Foot; ch 1, hdc in next 4 sc: 4 hdc.

Row 2: Ch 2, turn; (dc, ch 2, slip st) in first hdc, (slip st, ch 2, dc, ch 2, slip st) in each of next 2 hdc, slip st in last hdc; finish off.

FINISHING

Using Photo as a guide for placement and using long ends:

- Sew Belly to Body.
- Sew Wings on each side of Body, between Rnds 11 and 12.
- Sew Beak to Body above the Belly (between Eye Patch).
- Sew Feet to bottom of Body.
- Using satin stitch ***(Fig. 8, page 43)***, add Black eyes.

Designed by Linda A. Daley.

SHOPPING LIST

Yarn (Medium Weight)

- ☐ White - 45 yards (41 meters)
- ☐ Red - 10 yards (9 meters)
- ☐ Gold - 4 yards (3.7 meters)
- ☐ Black - 2 yards (1.8 meters)

Crochet Hooks

- ☐ Size G (4 mm)
  or size needed for gauge

Additional Supplies

- ☐ Polyester fiberfill
- ☐ Yarn needle

GAUGE INFORMATION

8 sc and 8 rows/rnds = 2" (5 cm)
Gauge Swatch: 2" (5 cm) square
Ch 9.
Row 1: Sc in second ch from hook and in each ch across: 8 sc.
Rows 2-8: Ch 1, turn; sc in each sc across.
Finish off.
Save time, check your gauge.

STITCH GUIDE

SINGLE CROCHET 2 TOGETHER
(abbreviated sc2tog)
Pull up a loop in each of next 2 sts, YO and draw through all 3 loops on hook **(counts as one sc)** ***(Fig. A)***.

Fig. A

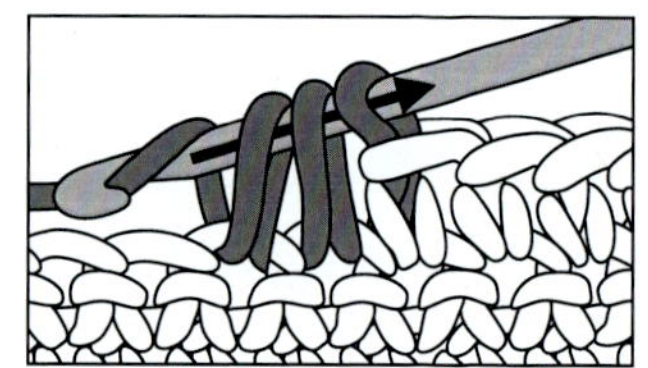

HEAD & BODY

Rnd 1 (Right side)**:** With White, make an adjustable ring, work 6 sc in ring ***(Figs. 3a-d, pages 40 & 41)***; do **not** join, place marker to indicate the beginning of the round ***(Fig. 1, page 40)***.

Note: Loop a short piece of yarn around any stitch to mark Rnd 1 as **right** side.

Rnd 2: 2 Sc in each sc around: 12 sc.

Rooster

EASY

Finished Height: Approx. 4½" (11.5 cm)

Rnd 3: (Sc in next sc, 2 sc in next sc) around: 18 sc.

Rnd 4: (2 Sc in next sc, sc in next 2 sc) around: 24 sc.

Rnd 5: Sc in each sc around.

Rnd 6: (Sc in next 5 sc, 2 sc in next sc) around: 28 sc.

Rnd 7: Sc in each sc around.

Rnd 8: (Sc in next 6 sc, 2 sc in next sc) around: 32 sc.

Rnds 9 and 10: Sc in each sc around.

Rnd 11: (2 Sc in next sc, sc in next 7 sc) around: 36 sc.

Rnds 12-15: Sc in each sc around.

Rnd 16: (Sc2tog, sc in next 7 sc) around: 32 sc.

Rnd 17: Sc in each sc around.

Rnd 18: (Sc in next 2 sc, sc2tog) around: 24 sc.

Rnd 19: Sc in each sc around.

Rnd 20: (Sc in next sc, sc2tog) around: 16 sc.

Rnd 21: Sc in each sc around.

Stuff piece with polyester fiberfill, shaping piece like an egg.

Rnd 22: Sc2tog around; slip st in next sc, finish off leaving an 8" (20.5 cm) length for sewing: 8 sts.

Thread yarn needle with end and weave yarn through Front Loop Only of remaining sts to close ***(Fig. 6, page 42)***; secure end.

WING (Make 2)

Rnd 1 (Right side)**:** With White, make an adjustable ring, work 6 sc in ring; do **not** join, place marker to indicate the beginning of the round.

Note: Mark Rnd 1 as **right** side.

Rnd 2: 2 Sc in each sc around: 12 sc.

Rnd 3: (Sc in next sc, 2 sc in next sc) around: 18 sc.

Wing Tip: (Hdc, dc) in next sc, 2 tr in next sc, ch 1, slip st in top of last tr made, 2 tr in same sc as previous tr, (dc, hdc) in next sc, sc in next sc, slip st in next sc; finish off leaving an 8" (20.5 cm) length for sewing.

BEAK

Rnd 1 (Right side)**:** With Gold, make an adjustable ring, work 4 sc in ring; do **not** join, place marker to indicate the beginning of the round.

Note: Mark Rnd 1 as **right** side.

Rnd 2: (2 Sc in next sc, sc in next sc) twice: 6 sc.

Rnd 3: (2 Sc in next sc, sc in next 2 sc) twice; slip st in next sc, finish off leaving an 8" (20.5 cm) length for sewing: 8 sts.

WATTLE

Rnd 1 (Right side)**:** With Red, make an adjustable ring; ch 3, (4 tr, ch 3, slip st, ch 3, 4 tr, ch 3, slip st) in ring; close ring **tightly**, finish off leaving an 8" (20.5 cm) length for sewing.

COMB

With Red, ch 8.

Row 1: Sc in second ch from hook and in each ch across: 7 sc.

Row 2: Ch 2, turn; (dc, 3 tr, dc, ch 2, slip st) in first sc, slip st in next sc, (slip st, ch 2, dc, 3 tr, dc, ch 2, slip st) in next sc, slip st in next sc, (slip st, ch 2, hdc, dc, tr, dc, hdc, ch 2, slip st) in next sc, slip st in next sc, (slip st, ch 1, sc, hdc, dc, hdc, sc, ch 1, slip st) in last sc; finish off leaving a 10" (25.5 cm) length for sewing.

FINISHING

Using Photo as a guide for placement and using long ends:

- Sew Wings on each side of Body.
- Sew Beak to center of face, across Rnds 10 and 11; sew Wattle below Beak.
- Sew Comb to center top of Head.
- Using satin stitch, add Black eyes across Rnds 9 and 10, having 4 sc between eyes *(**Fig. 8, page 43**)*.

Designed by Linda A. Daley.

SHOPPING LIST

Yarn (Medium Weight) MEDIUM 4

- ☐ White - 45 yards (41 meters)
- ☐ Grey - 12 yards (11 meters)
- ☐ Black - small amount

Crochet Hooks

- ☐ Size G (4 mm)
  or size needed for gauge

Additional Supplies

- ☐ Polyester fiberfill
- ☐ Yarn needle

STITCH GUIDE

SINGLE CROCHET 2 TOGETHER
(abbreviated sc2tog)
Pull up a loop in each of next 2 sts, YO and draw through all 3 loops on hook **(counts as one sc)** ***(Fig. A)***.

Fig. A

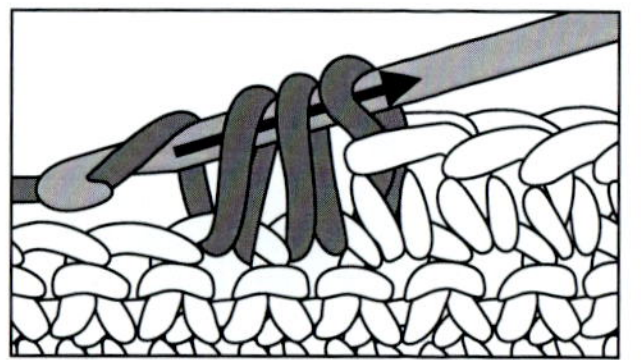

GAUGE INFORMATION

8 sc and 8 rows/rnds = 2" (5 cm)
Gauge Swatch: 2" (5 cm) square
Ch 9.
Row 1: Sc in second ch from hook and in each ch across: 8 sc.
Rows 2-8: Ch 1, turn; sc in each sc across.
Finish off.
Save time, check your gauge.

HEAD & BODY

Rnd 1 (Right side)**:** With White, make an adjustable ring, work 6 sc in ring ***(Figs. 3a-d, pages 40 & 41)***; do **not** join, place marker to indicate the beginning of the round ***(Fig. 1, page 40)***.

Note: Loop a short piece of yarn around any stitch to mark Rnd 1 as **right** side.

Lamb

EASY

Finished Height: Approx. 4" (10 cm)

Rnd 2: 2 Sc in each sc around: 12 sc.

Rnd 3: (Sc in next sc, 2 sc in next sc) around: 18 sc.

Rnd 4: (2 Sc in next sc, sc in next 2 sc) around: 24 sc.

Rnd 5: Sc in each sc around.

Rnd 6: (Sc in next 5 sc, 2 sc in next sc) around: 28 sc.

Rnd 7: Sc in each sc around.

Rnd 8: (Sc in next 6 sc, 2 sc in next sc) around: 32 sc.

Rnds 9 and 10: Sc in each sc around.

Rnd 11: (2 Sc in next sc, sc in next 7 sc) around: 36 sc.

Rnds 12-15: Sc in each sc around.

Rnd 16: (Sc2tog, sc in next 7 sc) around: 32 sc.

Rnd 17: Sc in each sc around.

Rnd 18: (Sc in next 2 sc, sc2tog) around: 24 sc.

Rnd 19: Sc in each sc around.

Rnd 20: (Sc in next sc, sc2tog) around: 16 sc.

Rnd 21: Sc in each sc around.

Stuff piece with polyester fiberfill, shaping piece like an egg.

Rnd 22: Sc2tog around; slip st in next sc, finish off leaving an 8" (20.5 cm) length for sewing: 8 sts.

Thread yarn needle with end and weave yarn through Front Loop Only of remaining sc to close ***(Fig. 6, page 42)***; secure end.

EAR (Make 2)

Rnd 1 (Right side)**:** With Grey, make an adjustable ring, work 5 sc in ring; do **not** join, place marker to indicate the beginning of round.

Note: Mark Rnd 1 as **right** side.

Rnd 2: 2 Sc in each sc around: 10 sc.

Rnd 3: (2 Sc in next sc, sc in next sc) around: 15 sc.

Rnds 4 and 5: Sc in each sc around.

Rnd 6: (Sc2tog, sc in next 3 sc) 3 times: 12 sc.

Rnd 7: (Sc2tog, sc in next 2 sc) 3 times; slip st in next sc, finish off leaving an 8" (20.5 cm) length for sewing: 9 sts.

TAIL

With Grey, ch 4; working in back ridge of chs *(Fig. 4, page 41)*, sc in second ch from hook, hdc in last 2 chs; finish off leaving a 6" (15 cm) length for sewing.

FINISHING

Using Photo as a guide for placement and using long ends:

Sew one Ear to each side of Head across Rnds 4 and 5.

Sew Tail across Rnds 16 and 17 at center back.

Using turkey loop stitch *(Fig. 12, page 44)*, add White loops to top of Head across Rnds 1-3.

Using satin stitch *(Fig. 8, page 43)*, add Black eyes across Rnds 7 and 8, having 3-4 sc between eyes.

Using a fly stitch *(Fig. 11, page 44)*, add facial features with Grey.

Designed by Linda A. Daley.

SHOPPING LIST

Yarn (Medium Weight) MEDIUM 4

- ☐ Pink - 60 yards (55 meters)
- ☐ Dk Pink - small amount
- ☐ Black - small amount

Crochet Hooks

- ☐ Size G (4 mm)
  or size needed for gauge

Additional Supplies

- ☐ Polyester fiberfill
- ☐ Yarn needle

STITCH GUIDE

SINGLE CROCHET 2 TOGETHER
(abbreviated sc2tog)

Pull up a loop in each of next 2 sts, YO and draw through all 3 loops on hook **(counts as one sc)** ***(Fig. A)***.

Fig. A

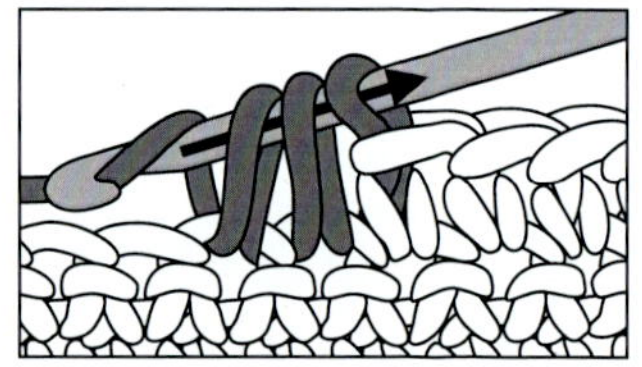

GAUGE INFORMATION

8 sc and 8 rows/rnds = 2" (5 cm)
Gauge Swatch: 2" (5 cm) square
Ch 9.
Row 1: Sc in second ch from hook and in each ch across: 8 sc.
Rows 2-8: Ch 1, turn; sc in each sc across.
Finish off.
Save time, check your gauge.

HEAD & BODY

Rnd 1 (Right side)**:** With Pink, make an adjustable ring, work 6 sc in ring ***(Figs. 3a-d, pages 40 & 41)***; do **not** join, place marker to indicate the beginning of the round ***(Fig. 1, page 40)***.

Note: Loop a short piece of yarn around any stitch to mark Rnd 1 as **right** side.

Rnd 2: 2 Sc in each sc around: 12 sc.

Piggy

EASY

Finished Height: Approx. 4" (10 cm)

Rnd 3: (Sc in next sc, 2 sc in next sc) around: 18 sc.

Rnd 4: (2 Sc in next sc, sc in next 2 sc) around: 24 sc.

Rnd 5: (Sc in next 5 sc, 2 sc in next sc) around: 28 sc.

Rnds 6-8: Sc in each sc around.

Rnd 9: (Sc in next 6 sc, 2 sc in next sc) around: 32 sc.

Rnds 10-12: Sc in each sc around.

Rnd 13: (2 Sc in next sc, sc in next 7 sc) around: 36 sc.

Rnds 14-16: Sc in each sc around.

Rnd 17: (Sc2tog, sc in next 7 sc) around: 32 sc.

Rnd 18: Sc in each sc around.

Rnd 19: (Sc in next 2 sc, sc2tog) around: 24 sc.

Rnd 20: Sc in each sc around.

Rnd 21: (Sc in next sc, sc2tog) around: 16 sc.

Rnd 22: Sc in each sc around.

Stuff piece with polyester fiberfill, shaping piece like an egg.

Rnd 23: Sc2tog around; slip st in next sc, finish off leaving an 8" (20.5 cm) length for sewing: 8 sts.

Thread yarn needle with end and weave yarn through Front Loops Only of remaining sc to close ***(Fig. 6, page 42)***; secure end.

EAR (Make 2)

With Pink and leaving a 10" (25.5 cm) length for sewing, ch 4.

Row 1 (Right side)**:** 2 Sc in second ch from hook, sc in next ch, 2 sc in last ch: 5 sc.

Note: Mark Row 1 as **right** side.

Row 2: Ch 1, turn; sc in first 2 sc, 2 sc in next sc, sc in last 2 sc: 6 sc.

Row 3: Ch 1, turn; sc in each sc across.

Row 4: Ch 1, turn; sc in first sc, sc2tog twice, sc in last sc: 4 sc.

Row 5: Ch 1, turn; sc in first sc, sc2tog, sc in last sc: 3 sc.

Row 6: Ch 1, turn; skip first sc, sc2tog; finish off: one sc.

SNOUT

Rnd 1 (Right side)**:** With Pink, make an adjustable ring, work 5 sc in ring; do **not** join, place marker to indicate the beginning of the round.

Note: Mark Rnd 1 as **right** side.

Rnd 2: 2 Sc in each sc around; slip st in next sc: 10 sts.

Rnd 3: Sc in Back Loop Only of same st as slip st and in each sc around ***(Fig. 6, page 42)***; do **not** join, place marker to indicate the beginning of the round: 10 sc.

Rnd 4: Working in both loops, sc in next sc, 2 sc in next sc, (sc in next 3 sc, 2 sc in next sc) twice; slip st in next sc, finish off leaving a 10" (25.5 cm) length for sewing.

TAIL

Ch 7; 3 sc in top loop of second ch from hook and each ch across; finish off leaving a 6" (15 cm) length for sewing.

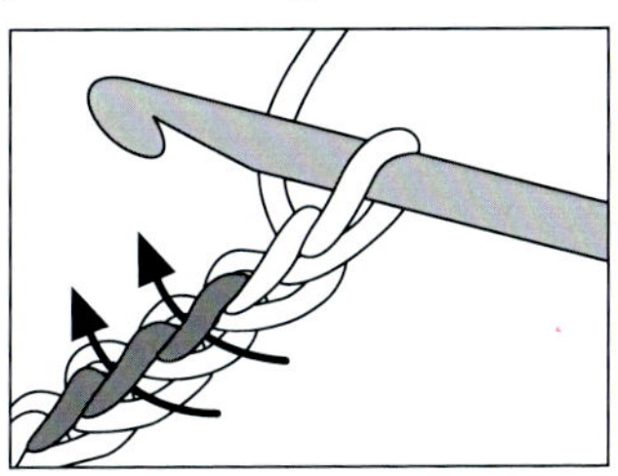

FINISHING

Using Photo as a guide for placement and using long ends:

- Sew one Ear to each side of Head across Rnds 4-6.
- Using straight stitch ***(Fig. 9, page 43)***, add Dk Pink Nostrils to Snout; sew Snout Face across Rnds 7-11, centering it between Ears.
- Sew Tail, centered on the back, across Rnds 18 and 19.
- Using satin stitch ***(Fig. 8, page 43)***, add Black eyes across Rnds 7 and 8, having 4 sts between eyes.

Designed by Linda A. Daley.

GENERAL INSTRUCTIONS

ABBREVIATIONS

ch(s)	chain(s)
cm	centimeters
dc	double crochet(s)
hdc	half double crochet(s)
mm	millimeters
Rnd(s)	Round(s)
sc	single crochet(s)
sc2tog	single crochet 2 together
st(s)	stitch(es)
tr	treble crochet(s)
YO	yarn over

SYMBOLS & TERMS

★ — work enclosed instructions **as many** times as indicated in addition to the first time.

( ) or **[ ]** — work enclosed instructions **as many** times as specified by the number immediately following **or** work all enclosed instructions in the stitch or space indicated **or** contains explanatory remarks.

colon (:) — the number(s) given after a colon at the end of a row or round denote(s) the number of stitches you should have on that row or round.

CROCHET TERMINOLOGY		
UNITED STATES		INTERNATIONAL
slip stitch (slip st)	=	single crochet (sc)
single crochet (sc)	=	double crochet (dc)
half double crochet (hdc)	=	half treble crochet (htr)
double crochet (dc)	=	treble crochet (tr)
treble crochet (tr)	=	double treble crochet (dtr)
double treble crochet (dtr)	=	triple treble crochet (ttr)
triple treble crochet (tr tr)	=	quadruple treble crochet (qtr)
skip	=	miss

BASIC	Projects using basic stitches. May include basic increases and decreases.
EASY	Projects may include simple stitch patterns, color work, and/or shaping.
INTERMEDIATE	Projects may include involved stitch patterns, color work, and/or shaping.
COMPLEX	Projects may include complex stitch patterns, color work, and/or shaping using a variety of techniques and stitches simultaneously.

GAUGE

Exact gauge is essential for proper size. Before beginning your project, make the sample swatch given in the instructions in the yarn and hook specified. After completing the swatch, measure it, counting your stitches and rows or rounds carefully. If your swatch is larger or smaller than specified, **make another, changing hook size to get the correct gauge**. Keep trying until you find the size hook that will give you the specified gauge.

Yarn Weight Symbol & Names	LACE 0	SUPER FINE 1	FINE 2	LIGHT 3	MEDIUM 4	BULKY 5	SUPER BULKY 6	JUMBO 7
Type of Yarns in Category	Fingering, size 10 crochet thread	Sock, Fingering, Baby	Sport, Baby	DK, Light Worsted	Worsted, Afghan, Aran	Chunky, Craft, Rug	Super Bulky, Roving	Jumbo, Roving
Crochet Gauge* Ranges in Single Crochet to 4" (10 cm)	32-42 sts**	21-32 sts	16-20 sts	12-17 sts	11-14 sts	8-11 sts	6-9 sts	5 sts and fewer
Advised Hook Size Range	Steel*** 6 to 8, Regular hook B-1	B-1 to E-4	E-4 to 7	7 to I-9	I-9 to K-10½	K-10½ to M/N-13	M/N-13 to Q	Q and larger

*GUIDELINES ONLY: The chart above reflects the most commonly used gauges and hook sizes for specific yarn categories.

** Lace weight yarns are usually crocheted with larger hooks to create lacy openwork patterns. Accordingly, a gauge range is difficult to determine. Always follow the gauge stated in your pattern.

*** Steel crochet hooks are sized differently from regular hooks–the higher the number, the smaller the hook, which is the reverse of regular hook sizing.

CROCHET HOOKS																	
U.S.	B-1	C-2	D-3	E-4	F-5	G-6	7	H-8	I-9	J-10	K-10½	L-11	M/N-13	N/P-15	P/Q	Q	S
Metric - mm	2.25	2.75	3.25	3.5	3.75	4	4.5	5	5.5	6	6.5	8	9	10	15	16	19

TO PLACE A MARKER

Markers are used to help distinguish the beginning of each round being worked. Place a 2" (5 cm) scrap piece of yarn before the first stitch of each round ***(Fig. 1)***, moving marker after each round is complete.

Fig. 1

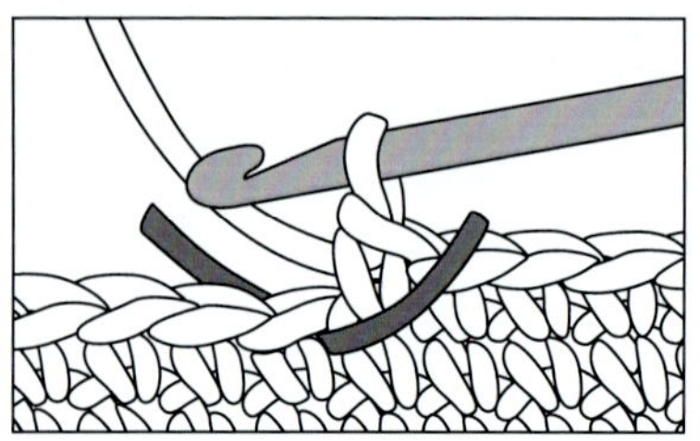

JOINING WITH A SC

Begin with a slip knot on hook. Insert hook in st indicated, YO and pull up a loop, YO and draw through both loops on hook ***(Fig. 2)***.

Fig. 2

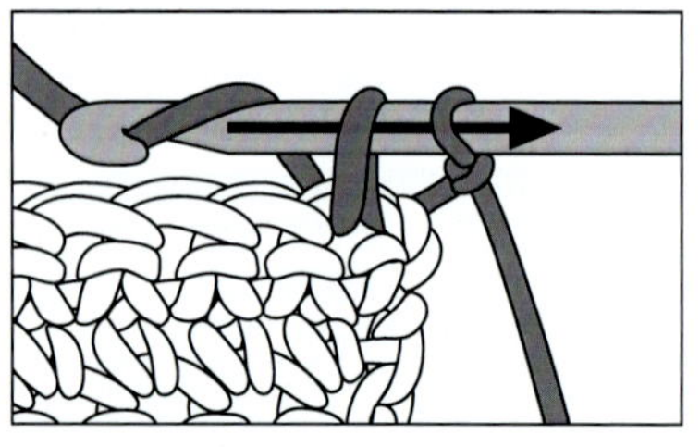

ADJUSTABLE RING

Wind the yarn around two fingers to form a ring ***(Fig. 3a)***.

Fig. 3a

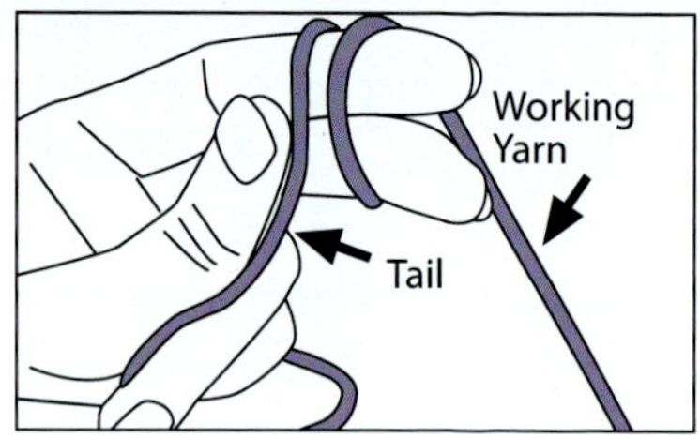

Slide the yarn off your fingers and grasp the strands at the top of the ring ***(Fig. 3b)***.

Fig. 3b

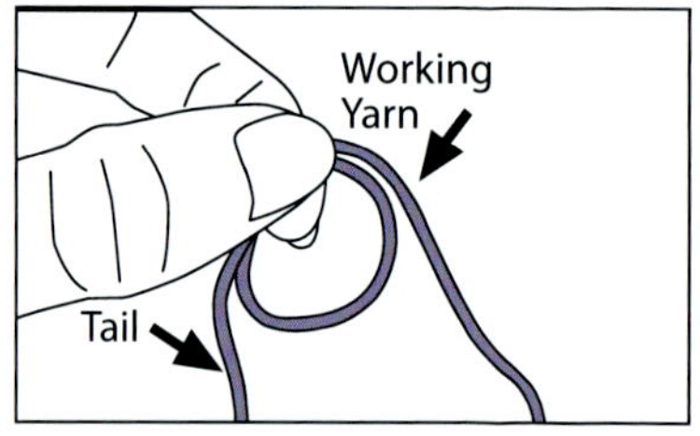

Insert the hook from **front** to **back** into the ring, pull up a loop, YO and draw through the loop on hook to lock the ring ***(Fig. 3c)***.

Fig. 3c

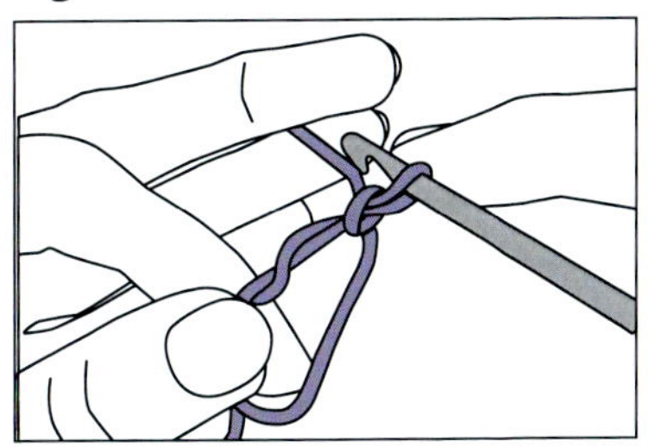

Working around both strands, work stitches in the ring as specified, then pull the yarn end to close ***(Fig. 3d)***.

Fig. 3d

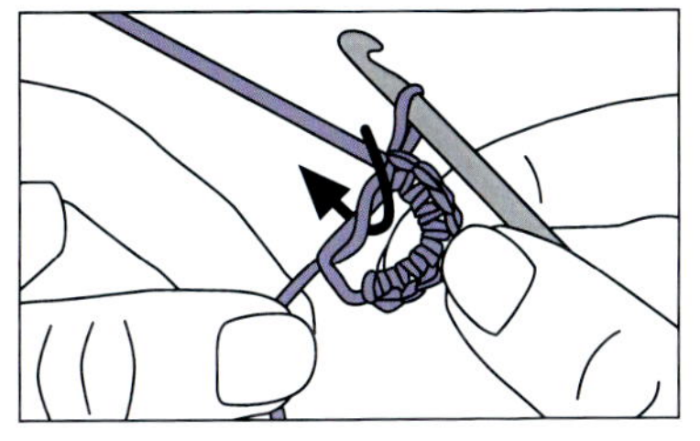

BACK RIDGE OF A CHAIN

Work in loops indicated by arrows ***(Fig. 4)***.

Fig. 4

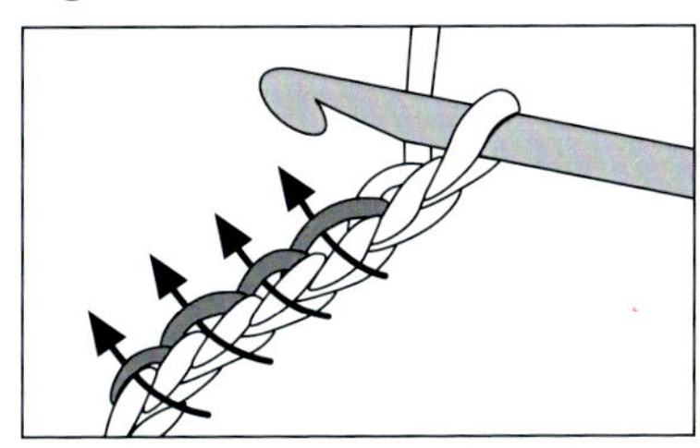

FREE LOOPS

After working in Back Loops Only on a round, there will be a ridge of unused loops. These are called the free loops. Later, when instructed to work in the free loops of the same round, work in these loops ***(Fig. 5a)***.

Fig. 5a

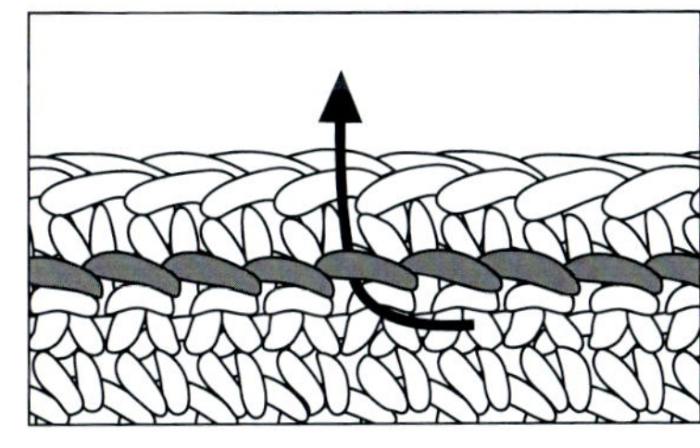

To work in free loops of a chain, work in loop indicated by arrow ***(Fig. 5b)***.

Fig. 5b

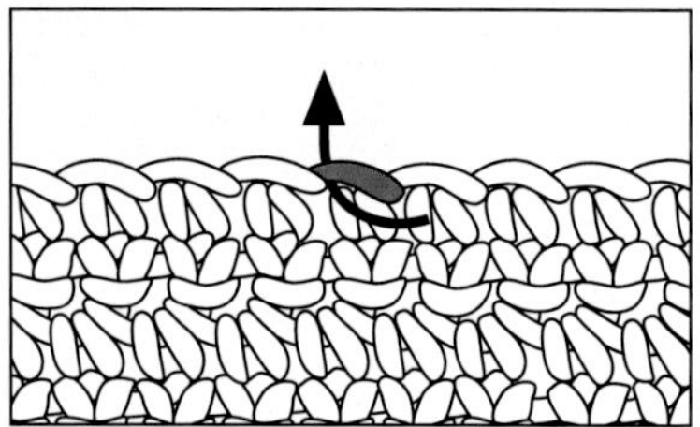

FRONT OR BACK LOOPS ONLY

Work in loop indicated by arrow ***(Fig. 6)***.

Fig. 6

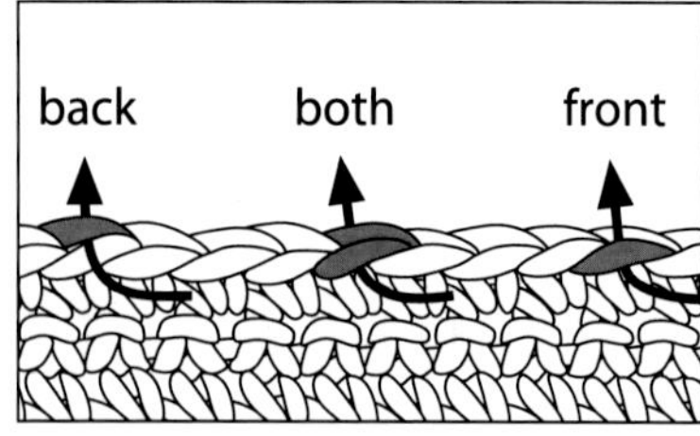

CHANGING COLORS

TO CHANGE COLORS IN LAST SC

Insert hook in sc indicated, YO and pull up a loop, drop yarn; with new color yarn, YO and draw through both loops on hook ***(Fig. 7a)***.

Fig. 7a

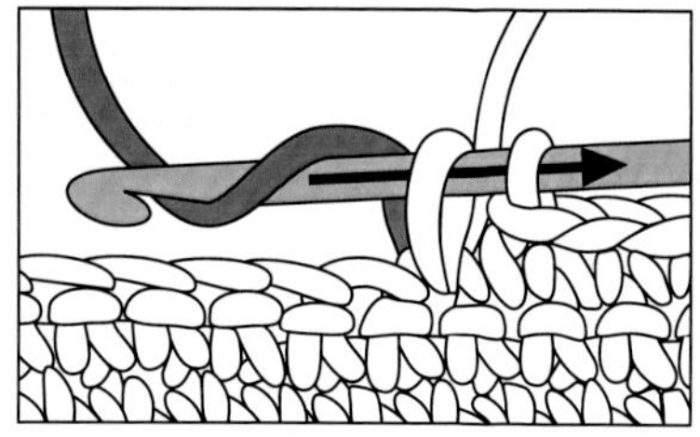

TO CHANGE COLORS IN LAST HDC

YO, insert hook in st indicated, YO and pull up a loop, drop old color, with new color, YO and draw through all 3 loops on hook ***(Fig. 7b)***.

Fig. 7b

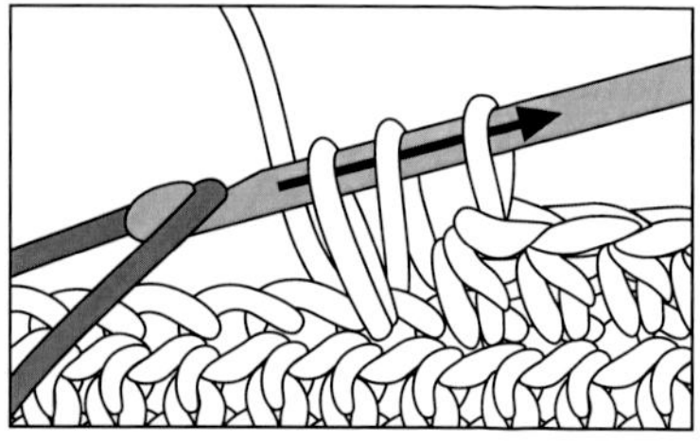

EMBROIDERY STITCHES

SATIN STITCH

Satin stitch is a series of straight stitches entering and exiting the same hole. Bring the needle up at 1 and go down at 2 ***(Fig. 8)***.

Fig. 8

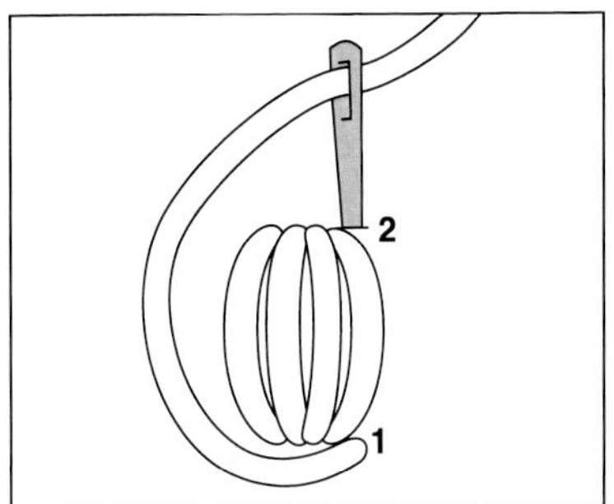

STRAIGHT STITCH

Straight stitch is just what the name implies, a single straight stitch. Come up at 1 and go down at 2 ***(Fig. 9)***.

Fig. 9

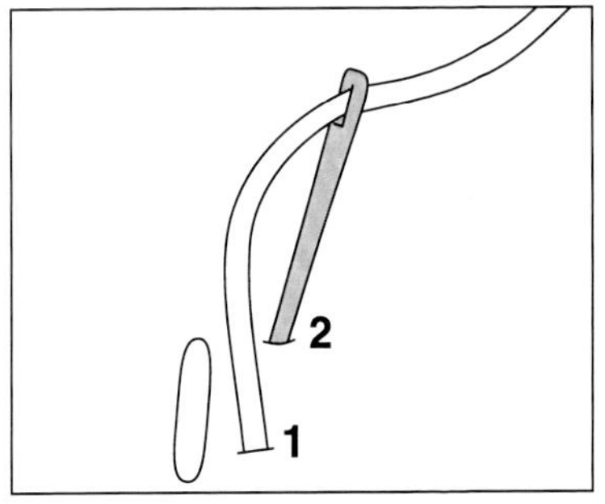

FRENCH KNOT

Bring needle up at 1. Wrap yarn around the needle the desired number of times and insert needle at 2, holding end of yarn with non-stitching fingers. Tighten knot; then pull needle through, holding yarn until it must be released ***(Fig. 10)***.

Fig. 10

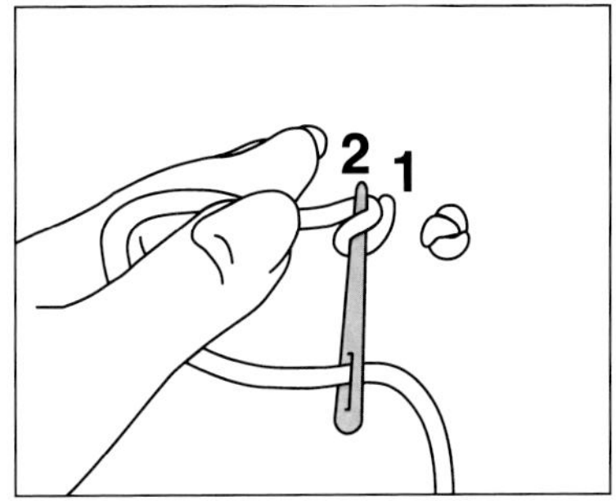

FLY STITCH

The fly stitch can be used to form a curved line from a straight line, holding it in place. Come up at 1, go down at 2, come up again at 3, and go down at 4 ***(Fig. 11)***.

Fig. 11

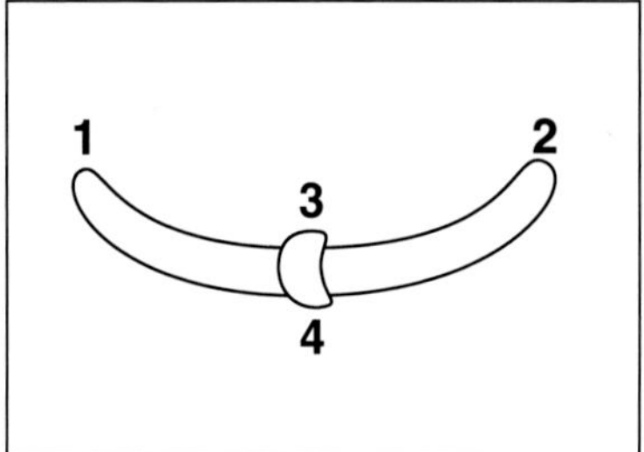

TURKEY LOOP STITCH

Bring the needle up at 1 and go down at 2 leaving a ¾ in. (1.9 cm) loop, come up at 3 and go down at 4 to secure loop ***(Fig. 12)***. Repeat for each loop.

Fig. 12

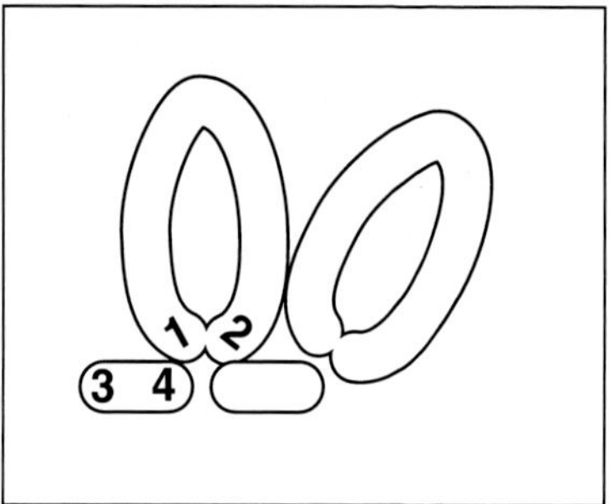

BASIC CROCHET STITCHES

SLIP STITCH

Insert hook in stitch indicated, YO and draw through stitch and through loop on hook ***(Fig. 13) (abbreviated slip st)***.

Fig. 13

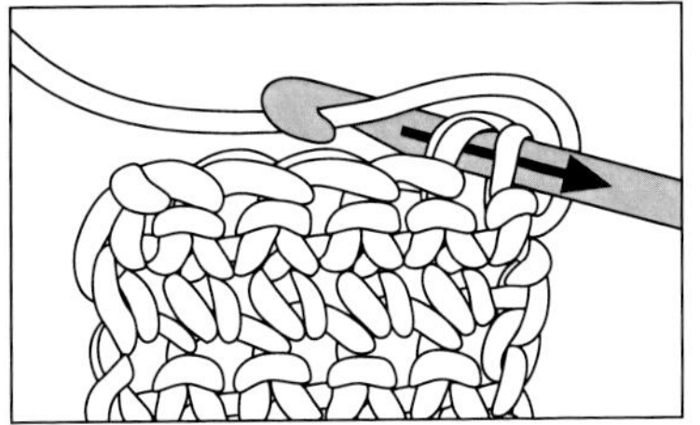

HALF DOUBLE CROCHET

YO, insert hook in stitch indicated, YO and pull up a loop, YO and draw through all 3 loops on hook ***(Fig. 15) (abbreviated hdc)***.

Fig. 15

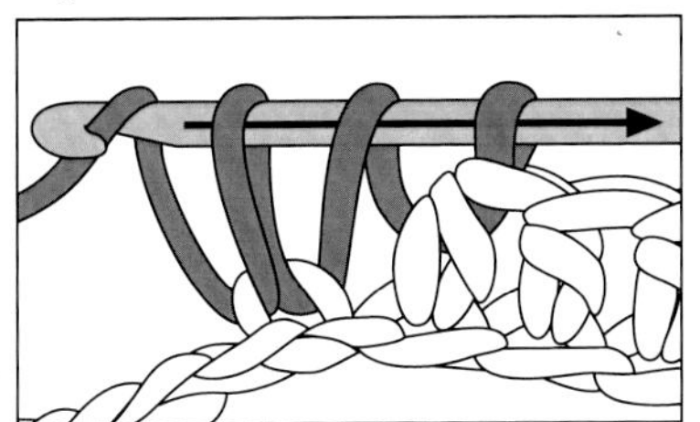

SINGLE CROCHET

Insert hook in stitch indicated, YO and pull up a loop, YO and draw through both loops on hook ***(Fig. 14) (abbreviated sc)***.

Fig. 14

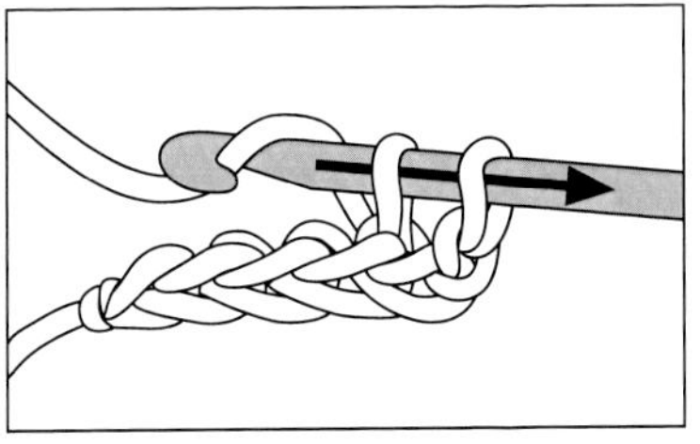

DOUBLE CROCHET

YO, insert hook in stitch indicated, YO and pull up a loop (3 loops on hook), YO and draw through 2 loops on hook ***(Fig. 16a)***, YO and draw through remaining 2 loops on hook ***(Fig. 16b) (abbreviated dc)***.

Fig. 16a

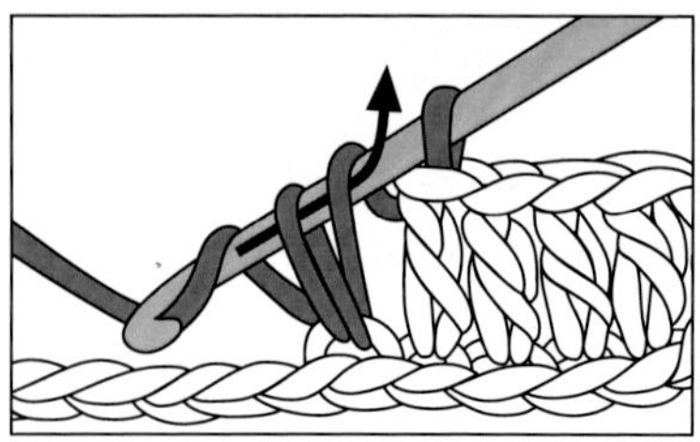

Fig. 16b

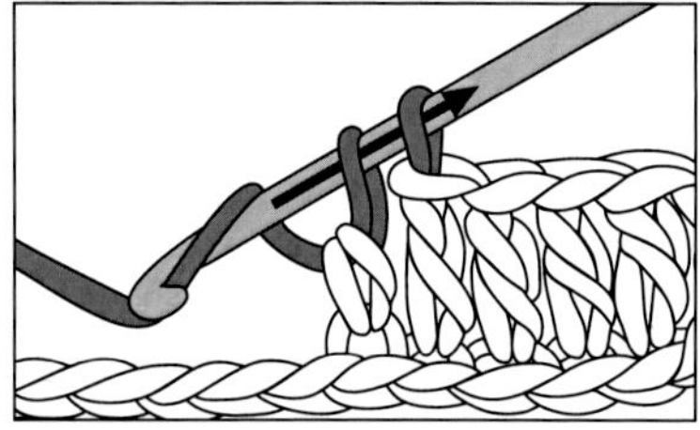

TREBLE CROCHET

YO twice, insert hook in stitch indicated, YO and pull up a loop (4 loops on hook) ***(Fig. 17a)***, (YO and draw through 2 loops on hook) 3 times ***(Fig. 17b) (abbreviated tr)***.

Fig. 17a

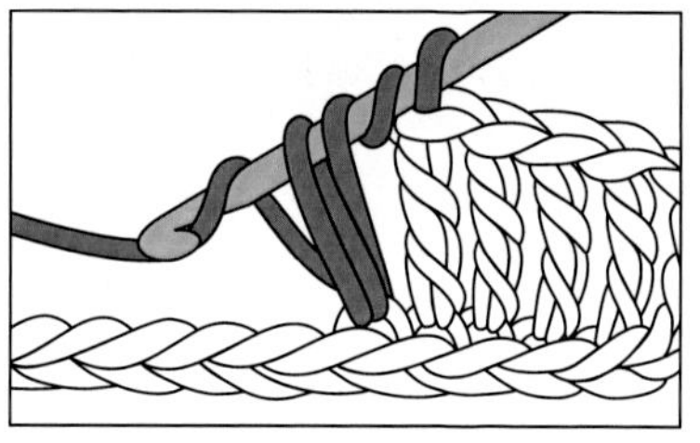

Fig. 17b

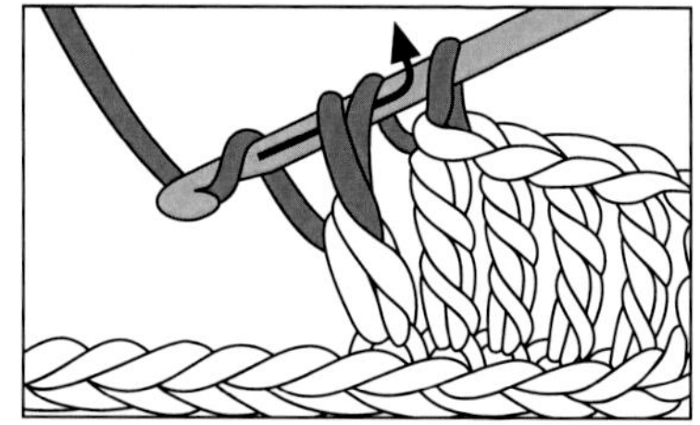

YARN INFORMATION

Each Pudgie in this book was made using ***Red Heart® Super Saver®***, a Medium Weight Yarn. Any brand of Medium Weight yarn may be used. Remember, to arrive at the finished size, it is the GAUGE/TENSION that is important.

For your convenience, listed below are the specific colors used to create our photography models. Because yarn manufacturers make frequent changes to their product lines, you may sometimes find it necessary to use a substitute yarn or to search for the discontinued product at alternate suppliers (locally or online).

LADYBUG
Black - #0312 Black
Red - #0319 Cherry Red
White - #0311 White

BEE
Yellow - #0320 Cornmeal
Black - #0312 Black
White - #311 White

BIRDY
Brown - #0360 Café Latte
Red - #0319 Cherry Red
Yellow - #0320 Cornmeal
Black - #0312 Black

EAGLE
Brown - #0360 Café Latte
White - #0311 White
Yellow - #0320 Cornmeal
Black - #0312 Black

PENGUIN
Black - #0312 Black
White - #0311 White
Gold - #0234 Saffron

ROOSTER
White - #0311 White
Red - #0319 Cherry Red
Gold - #0234 Saffron
Black - #0312 Black

LAMB
White - #0316 Soft White
Grey - #0400 Grey Heather
Black - #0312 Black

PIGGY
Pink - #0373 Petal Pink
Dk Pink - #0774 Light Raspberry
Black - #0312 Black

We have made every effort to ensure that these instructions are accurate and complete. we cannot, however, be responsible for human error, typographical mistakes, or variations in individual work.

Made in U.S.A.